© Fayer

Archibald MacLeish

Mr. MacLeish's most recent book, *Collected Poems 1917-1952*, was honored by the award of the Pulitzer and Bollingen prizes, the Shelley Memorial Award, and the National Book Award.

"Archibald MacLeish's 'Collected Poems' is a major achievement in American letters . . . a total impact of strong intellectual poise, widespread ability with verse forms, and great lyrical charm."

New York Times

"To possess all of this distinguished poet's work in one volume makes possible a new experience." *Perspectives USA*

"The 'Collected Poems' of Archibald MacLeish is a major work . . . The masculinity of his lines, the magnificent rhythms of his blank verse, his terza rima adaptations, his technical accomplishments in many verse forms, and his perfection in the use of simple iambics are paradigms of excellence." *Saturday Review*

SONGS

BY

 : HOUGHTON MIFFLIN COMPANY

FOR EVE

ARCHIBALD M<small>A</small>cLEISH

BOSTON : THE RIVERSIDE PRESS CAMBRIDGE :

TWENTY-ONE POEMS

vi

SONGS FOR EVE

1. WHAT EVE SANG

Space-time
Is all there is of space and time
But is not all. There is a rhyme
For all of space and all of time.

I heard it on that Eden night
The branching tree stood dark alight
Like willow in the wind, so white
Its unknown apples on the night:

I heard beyond that tree a tree
Stir in silence over me.
In space and time, eyes only see,
Ears only hear, the green-wood tree:

But Oh! I heard the whole of time
And all of space give ringing rhyme
And ring and ring and chime and chime
When I reached out to touch and climb
In spite of space, in spite of time.

Eve said:
From tree to tree
Will journey be;
The one, she said,
Alive and green,
The other dead,
And what's between,
Eve said,
Our lives mean.

Eve said:
With tree began
That traveller, man;
With tree, she said,
Will journey end.
That tree, though dead,
Its leaves will spend,
Eve said,
World without end.

Eve said:
The first is his
Whose world this is:
The last, she said,
Blossomed and blown
Though wood be dead,
Is mine, my own.
Eve said:
O my son! O my son!

3. WHAT ADAM SAID

My life began
Not when I was moulded man
But when beneath the apple tree
I saw what none but I could see:
Adam flesh and Adam bone
And Adam by himself alone.

That day he sees
His own two hands, those mysteries —
His flesh, his bone and yet not his —
That day man knows himself, and is.

4. WHAT THE GREEN TREE SAID

Wakening is forbidden
To all in space and time —
Star and stone, bird and beast.

Wakers see what sleep has hidden.
Wakers will no longer rest
In space and time as they were bidden.

Eden was an endless place,
Time enough for all of space
And space for all that time to pass.

We lived in time as fishes live
Within the lapsing of the wave
That with the water's moving move.

We lived in space as hawk in air:
The place we were was everywhere
And everywhere we were, we were.

Fish and hawk have eyes of glass
Wherein the skies and waters pass
As in a glass the images —

They mirror but they may not see.
When I had tasted fruit of tree
Fish and hawk, they fled from me:

"She has a watcher in her eyes,"
The hawk screamed from the steep of skies,
Fish from sea-deep where he lies.

Our exile is our eyes that see.
Hawk and fish have eyes but we
Behold what they can only be.

Space within its time revolves
But Eve must spin as Adam delves
Because our exile is ourselves.

What did I eat when I ate apple?
What did I eat in the sweet
Day, in the leaves' dapple?
Eve.

What did I know when I knew apple?
What did I know in the new
Night, in the stars' stipple?
Eve.

7. WHAT THE VINE SAID TO EVE

Man is the leaky bung
That lets the ferment in:
The wine were sweet and young
But for your sin.

But for your fault the wine
Were sweet as water is:
No taint of taste, no sign,
No promises.

But for your sin no tongue
Had tasted, salt as blood,
The certainty among
These grapes of God.

              said Eve;
That Fall began
What leaves conceive
Nor fishes can —
So far a flight
Past touch, past sight.

Get down, said Eve
Upon your shins,
Upon your shanks,
And pray reprieve,
And give God thanks
For Eden sins.

The Fall! she said —
From earth to God!
Give thanks, said she, for branch, for bole,
For Eve who found the grace to fall
From Adam, browsing animal,
Into the soaring of the soul!

9. EVE'S NOW-I-LAY-ME

To separate myself from space
I gave the water pool my face:
To separate myself from time
I gave the stars my soul to climb.

10. ADAM IN THE EVENING

Beauty cannot be shown
But only at remove:
What's beautiful is known
By opposites, as love.

Counter, the mind can see.
When first Eve disobeyed
And turned and looked at me,
Beauty was made.

That distance in the blood
Whereby the eyes have sight
Is love — not understood
But infinite.

11. EVE IN THE DAWN

Time created out of clay
That animal with whom I lay.

Like she of wolf or lion's she
In season he would tumble me,

Yet touched me never till he took
The apple from my hand and Look!

Look! he said, your eyes that see
My eyes have images of me!

That night until the next of day
We touched in love and loving lay:

We were awake then who had slept.
Our bodies out of Eden leapt

Together to a lifted place
Past space of time and time of space

That neither space nor time had made.
There first we laughed, were first afraid.

Was it Adam, only he,
Bred that flowering branch of me
Whereon shall hang eternity?

Does anyone know, says Eve, that fable
Women in their dotage tell
Of girls covered by gods, unable
Afterward to call the babe?
What pipped and tapped in Leda's shell
Laid by the shoal there in the fable?

The soul that comes from God, one says,
And one remembers him as swan
Because the swan has feathery ways,
And one as bull, so brisk the blaze,
But none remembers him as man.
It was a man took me, Eve says.

Women, when a child is found,
Make the sea sound: Hush! Hush!
Does anyone know why they make that sound?
Our blood is salt as the sea around,
Our body, at each beginning, fish:
Hush! says Eve, when a child is found.

13. ADAM'S JEALOUSY:
EVE'S ANSWER

Cover that infant's mouth and eyes,
Said Adam, softly where it lies:
The soul that lurks, the soul that flies,
Will enter where it clucks and cries.

Hold close, said Adam, in the leaves,
That struggling girl who first conceives.
The souls are fluttering at the eaves:
They enter flesh when flesh believes.

The invisible souls, now Eden's lost,
Hunt, he said, the chosen host
To house them, body sick with ghost.
I fear the souls, said Adam, most.

Adam, Adam, there are none
Enter flesh but flesh and bone.

Flesh and bone have wonder done
And wonder, bone and flesh are One.

Raddle me riddle,
I'll spell you the word:
Two are together
And still there's a third
Mingles to meddle
Beneath the green tree:
One is its father,
One is its mother. . . .

What's born of three?

15. THE SERPENT'S RIDDLE

Riddle me raddle,
I'll tell you another:
The worm is its father,
The apple its mother,
It couples astraddle
But thinks it is moth
That on heavenly wing
Can fly and can fling.

What is it? . . . And why?

Raddle me riddle
Or weep if you'd rather.
Adam's its father,
Eve is its mother,
Yet where in the middle
There grows the green tree
Eve must take apple
Before it can be.

What is it? Ah me!

Riddle me raddle
And tell me the weather:
What wakes in a cradle
As light as a feather
And fallen from where?
What clings to its mother,
Its hand in her hair,
But stares at that other?

What knows its own father?

Who said you were bred
Not of flesh and of bone
But of somebody flown
From a place in the sky
Had no thew and no thigh
And no pelt and no poll?
Who told you that lie
About body and soul?

You think it was I,
Not that girl in the tower,
Was had by a shower
Of gold from the sky?
We do what we can!
There was none lay with me
But was made like a man
As a man ought to be.

You came by the soul
As you came by the skin
Where the raging strikes in
And the wrestlers must roll.
If you'd rather be more
You can brag if you'd rather:
Make your mother a whore,
Have a ghost for a father.

But O, the noon day
And O, the green tree!
Body of me
In the fern where we lay!
The flight that was flown
From the place in the sky —
The flesh and the bone
Made those wings that could fly.

19. WHAT THE SERPENT SAID
TO ADAM

Which is you, old two-in-one?
Which is which, old one of two?
When the doubling is undone
Which one is you?

Is it you that so delights
By that woman in her bed?
Or you the glimmering sky afrights,
Vast overhead?

Are you body, are you ghost?
Were you got or had no father?
Is this you — the guest? — the host?
Who then's the other?

That woman says, old one-of-two,
In body was the soul begun:
Now two are one and one is you: —
Which one? Which one?

20. WHAT THE LION SAID
TO THE CHILD

The flesh they say is stronger
And brisk with brutal blood;
The spirit mild and meekly made and good:
And spirit shuns the fight but should no longer,
For the flesh must be withstood,
So fell its lust, so foul its hunger.

If those that teach were fewer
And truer what they taught
A child might learn what fight is really fought
And which is lamb, which lion, of those two.
A child might learn, when prey is caught,
Flesh is not the fierce pursuer.

21. EVE QUIETS HER CHILDREN

Eve, our mother, care and keep!
We who call you cannot sleep.

Wake then! Weep!

Eve, our mother, all the rest
Sleep about us, bird and beast.

Waking's best.

All things other turn and twine
Like gnats in atmospheres of wine.

Eden's sign!

Stars that circle in their sleep
Silver solemn statutes keep.

Stars! Time's sheep!

Suns and moons and nails and claws
Sleep out time's revolving laws.

Time! Time was!

Eve, our mother, what was wrought
Broke the sleep when we were got?

Sleep's green tree was cut, was cut.

Eve, Eve, who are we,
Born to wake and waking see?

Wake and see!

You are the children of Eve by the apple.
By the pip of the apple she came to conceive.
Adam, that cuckold, never begot you.
You are the children of Eve
By the apple.

Adam was hot
In the heat of the day,
And he lay in her lap
And she gave him his way,
But the pip of the apple
I taught her to eat
(Tart? — sweet!)
Was quick in her womb.
When Adam came knocking
The inn had no room.

Said the king to the cock:
When the day comes to bloom
Be quiet for once!
I must sleep in the tomb.
Said the king to the huntsman:
Quiet your horn!
Let the day begin dumb:
There is sleep to be born.
But the pip of the apple
Was quick in his blood:
Eve's children can sleep
But not well — not for good.

23. EVE TO THE STORM OF THUNDER

Who teaches child that snivelling guilt
For space rejected and time spilt?
Tell me, how was Heaven built?

Space and time I disobeyed:
It was so that he was made,
Little man so fast afraid.

Had I not, in wonder's awe,
Disobeyed the lion's law,
Voice and hand were shriek and paw.

Had I not, for wonder's sake,
Broken law no leaf may break,
Lids were closed that now awake.

Only when I disobeyed
Was the bliss of Eden stayed —
Bliss of sleep in that thick shade.

Was it shame and was it sin,
Shameful out and shameless in,
So in waking to begin?

How else can heavenly thunder shake
The heart but if the heart awake?

The taste of time is sweet at first,
Then salt as tears, then tame as water:
Time to the old tastes bitter, bitter.

No child of mine may quench his thirst
However deep he drink of time,
Sweet or bitter, salt or tame.

Because my tongue that apple durst
His tongue shall want what time is not —
Not tame, not bitter, salt nor sweet:

Because my tongue that apple durst
Eternity shall be his thirst.

God who made the garden green
Made the apple tree to lean
And glitter in that shine and sheen.

The apple tree will fall away.

Straight of bole and strict of bough,
Sons of mine will shape and hew
Tree that Eden never knew.

The dry tree branch will swing and sway.

All to this my sons are born:
To hew and shape and raise that tree,
And stand beneath in scorn, in scorn . . . .
And on it bear eternity.

The apple tree shall fall away.

The dry tree branch shall swing and sway.

This sun at last will stand and stare
And blaze and burn its planets out,
And all God's works of skill and care
Will strew the starry sky about,
Yet hearts remain what once they were.

When nothing lives of all this light
But, somewhere between star and star,
A greater darkness on the night
Where once our glimmering signals were,
What heart has seen will still be sight.

Eden's tree will wither up,
And char and in its ashes drift,
But not one leaf will wilt or drop
From that dry tree my children lift
To bear the heart's rebellious hope.

27. EVE EXPLAINS TO THE THRUSH
WHO REPEATS EVERYTHING

(1)

On the first tree,
The green tree,
Mystery
Created me.

    On first tree grew
    Whereby I knew,
    Struck by that wonder's wonder through:
    Stricken and knew.

        Apple eaten of that tree
        Animal I ceased to be.

On the last tree,
The dry tree,
Eternity
My fruit shall be:

    On last be hung
    Whereby my tongue
    Shall sing and all the stars among
    Meaning be sung.

        Apple eaten of that tree
        Time itself shall cease to be.

Green tree,
Time's tree,
Mystery.

> By time was made
> The sheen, the shade,
> The fruit that in my mouth betrayed
> All that time made.

>> Apple eaten of that tree
>> Eve I was — and Eve might be.

Dry tree,
Man's tree,
Eternity.

> By man, his hand,
> That tree shall stand,
> And hold so still time's stars — so stand
> The world will end.

>> Apple eaten of that tree
>> Eve and thrush shall cease — and be.

28.   WHAT THE WIND SAID TO THE WATER:
WHAT THE WATER REPLIED

Man, like any creature,
Dies where two days meet:
Dead, by time is eaten.

> *Sea worm leaves behind*
> *Shell for wave to find:*
> *Man, the shell of mind.*

Like any creature, man
Lives by luck and vanishes:
The chance wind takes the candle.

> *No creature leaves behind*
> *Husk or shell or rind*
> *Obdurate as the mind.*

Life is luck, death random.
> *Tell me, what is man*
> *That immortal order can?*

TWENTY-ONE POEMS

THE INFINITE REASON

(1)

Rilke thought it was the human part
To translate planet into angel —
Bacteria of mortal heart

Fermenting, into something rich and strange,
The orchard at home, the sky above Toledo:
Sight into soul was what we lived to change.

The key, he told us, was the angel's need,
Not our necessity — and yet
No angel answered for *his* heart to feed.

(2)

The truth is nearer to the true than that.
The truth is, the necessity is ours.
Man is creature to whom meaning matters.

Until we read these faces, figures, flowers,
These shapes averted from us that all vanish,
Everything vanishes — a swarm of hours

Swirling about a bonfire that began
When? Why? To end where? And for what?

(3)

Miser of meanings in the stars, O man

Who finds the poem moonlight has forgotten!
Eternity is what our wanderers gather,
Image by image, out of time — the cut

Branch that flowers in the bowl. Our Father,
Thou who ever shalt be, the poor body
Dying at every ditch hath borne Thee, Father.

(4)

Our human part is to redeem the god
Drowned in this time of space, this space
That time encloses.

              From the Tyrrhenian flood

The floated marble, the cold human face!

Know the world by heart
Or never know it!
Let the pedant stand apart —
Nothing he can name will show it:
Also him of intellectual art.
None know it
Till they know the world by heart.

Take heart then, poet!

DR. SIGMUND FREUD
DISCOVERS THE SEA SHELL

for Harry Murray

Science, that simple saint, cannot be bothered
Figuring what anything is for:
Enough for her devotions that things are
And can be contemplated soon as gathered.

She knows how every living thing was fathered,
She calculates the climate of each star,
She counts the fish at sea, but cannot care
Why any one of them exists, fish, fire or feathered.

Why should she? Her religion is to tell
By rote her rosary of perfect answers.
Metaphysics she can leave to man:
She never wakes at night in heaven or hell

Staring at darkness. In her holy cell
There is no darkness ever: the pure candle
Burns, the beads drop briskly from her hand.

Who dares to offer Her the curled sea shell!
She will not touch it! — knows the world she sees
Is all the world there is! Her faith is perfect!

And still he offers the sea shell . . . .

What surf
Of what far sea upon what unknown ground
Troubles forever with that asking sound?
What surge is this whose question never ceases?

REPLY TO MR. WORDSWORTH

(1)

The flower that on the pear-tree settles
Momentarily as though a butterfly — that petal,
Has it alighted on the twig's black wet

From elsewhere? No, but blossoms from the bole:
Not traveller but the tree itself unfolding.
What of that stranger in the eyes, the soul?

(2)

Space-time, our scientists tell us, is impervious.
It neither evades nor refuses. It curves
As a wave will or a flame — whatever's fervent.

Space-time has no beginning and no end.
It has no door where anything can enter.
How break and enter what will only bend?

(3)

Must there be elsewhere too — not merely here —
To justify the certainty of miracles?
Because we cannot hope or even fear

For ghostly coming on the midnight hour,
Are there no women's eyes all ardor now
And on the tree no momentary flower?

INFILTRATION OF THE UNIVERSE

To William Empson

*"The ascent toward consciousness is the
'unnatural' thing in nature." Erich Neumann*

The liverfluke provides
The absolute analogy.
The fluke can neither leaf nor flower:
His habitat is guts and blood:
And yet the vegetable universe
Accepts him in the cockle of the snail
To share with tansy and with purse
Their herbal hour
And on the muncher of the grass prevail.
Like fluke made snail
So soul made flesh.
The universe of hoof and tail
Admits, concealed in flesh and bone,
The immortal wish
Whereby suns sicken and eternity is sown.

Why do they ring that bell
Twelve times in the steeple?

> To say the hill has swung —
> Houses and church and people,
> All of them fast asleep —
> To this place in time where the bell
> Tilts to its iron tongue
> Twelve times in the steeple.

Houses and hill don't care
Nor sleepers fast asleep.

> But the steeple says to the star:
> Here in the night we are,
> Hill and houses and men.
> Andromeda's shivering light,
> Orion's distant flare,
> Here we are in the night,
> Here we go by again.
> We go by you again says the bell,
> Again, says the bell, again. . . .

At twenty, stooping round about,
I thought the world a miserable place,
Truth a trick, faith in doubt,
Little beauty, less grace.

Now at sixty what I see,
Although the world is worse by far,
Stops my heart in ecstasy.
God, the wonders that there are!

WHY THE FACE OF THE CLOCK
IS NOT TRULY A CIRCLE

Time is not gone,
Time does not go,
Time can be found again
Old men know
If you travel a journey.

Paris again
And that scent in the air,
That sound in the street,
And the time is still there
At the end of the journey.

Turn at the door
Climb the stone stair —
What fragrance is that
In the dark, on the air,
At the end of the journey?

Time does not go:
Time keeps its place.
But oh the brown hair
And oh the bright face!
Where? By what journey?

Fish has laid her succulent eggs
Safe in Saragossa weed
So wound and bound that crabbed legs
Nor clattering claws can find and feed.

Thus fish commits unto the sea
Her infinite future and the Trade
Blows westward toward eternity
The universe her love has made.

But when, upon this leeward beach,
The measureless sea journey ends
And ball breaks open, from the breach
A deft, gold, glossy crab extends

In ring-side ritual of self-applause
The small ironic silence of his claws.

THE WOOD DOVE AT SANDY SPRING

Dove that lets the silence answer
Time after time the asking voice,
Trusting stillness as sweet dancer
Trusts to the music all her choice,

Dove that lets the music fall
Note after note into the silence,
Dove, ah dove, we also call:
Shall we learn silence in a while?

ST. PHILIP'S CHURCH IN ANTIGUA

for John Cowles

I think these empty pews are not deserted
Even though the ocean wind
Sings to itself as though they were,
And the blinds rattle. Here in the West Indies

Women, when they learn that lonely music,
Learn to hide their heart-beats from each other.
There might be kneeling women in these pews
Although the wandering wind touched nothing.

I think dead English women come here.
This church was all they had of England —
This and the hymn-tunes and the prayers:

They never called the island home,
But here, however the wood blinds might swing
And the wind cry, all the house was theirs.

FOR THE ANNIVERSARY OF
MY MOTHER'S DEATH

You think a life can end?
Mind knows, nor soul believes
How far, how far beyond
The shattering of the waves,
How deep within the land,
The surge of sea survives.

There is no least sea sound
Along these inland coves
Where the last waters ground,
Yet something, lapsing, leaves
Slow silver on the sand:
The wave still lifts. It lives.

Those surgings never end
Where salt sea water moves.
Not even, locked in land,
Is sea-beat still: it laves
The last, far-off, profound
Dark shore and deepest caves.

Silver in the wall of wave
The myriad small fish, before them
Smother of the crashing sea,
Behind them the Jacks, the Crevalli, the Barracuda.

Silver between death and death
Within the green clear glass, the cresting
Wave before the wave breaks, myriads:
Ai! between the death and death the silver!

What will our reputations be?
Whole things? Constructions
Resisting time (that sea!)
With the rock's persistent luck?

I doubt it. We leave behind
An anthological rubble:
Mind mingled with mind,
Odd and even coupled.

But poetry thrives that way.
Out of the tumbled coral
One exquisite spray,
Ivory, tipped with ore.

Who puts off shift
Has love's concealment left.

Who puts off skin
Has pain to wind her in.

Who puts off flesh
Wears soul's enormous wish.

Who puts off bone
Has all of death for gown.

None go naked who have drawn this breath
Till love's put off and pain and wish and death.

POET

for Ernest Hemingway

                 There must be
Moments when we see right through
Although we say we can't. I knew
A fisher who could lean and look
Blind into dazzle on the sea
And strike into that fire his hook,
Far under, and lean back and laugh
And let the line run out, and reel
What rod could weigh nor line could feel —
The heavy silver of his wish,
And when the reel-spool faltered, kneel
And with a fumbling hand that shook
Boat, all bloody from the gaff,
A shivering fish.

The fly against the window pane
That flings itself in flightless flight,
So it loves light,
Will die of love and die in vain.

Prisoner of the open wall
Where freedom is but turning round,
Still is it bound:
Love barred, there is no way at all.

My heart against the hard rib bone
Beat like a fly and would not be:
It had gone free
But that the shining world so shone.

What islands known, what passages discovered,
Rocks seen from far off to leeward,
Low, a few palms, odor of sandalwood,
The whole thing blue with dusk. . . .

Mostly I have relinquished and forgotten
Or grown accustomed, which is a way of forgetting.
The more I have travelled the less I have departed.
I had foreseen the unicorn, the nose-rings.

Once in my youth I bailed ship and launched her
As a blue-jay bolts from an apple-tree.
Now I go but have not gone:
Troy is Ithaca again but farther.

Only the young, on a first voyage, facing the
Whole horizon of the sea
Depart from any country. The old men
Sail to the sea-beach they have left behind.

shoaled on this shingle,
Beached by the ebbed age, grounded. . . .

If you want spectacles, WE are a spectacle!
The living lot, the generation,
Poking around in pools on the mudflat,
Kicking at clams, cokes, condoms,
Dead fish, minute animalcula,
Ear cocked to the long, withdrawing
Gurgle out of a ketchup bottle
Sucked by the descending silt. . . .

Where are the fountains of the deep, the fountains?
Where are the springs of the sea to enter them?

The ship fast and the fools everywhere!

Fools off in the muck to the eastward
Waiting for history to flood
On the date set by the Central Praesidium:
A tide in the affairs of men
Fixed by the water-works, a fraudulent
Season of the sea. . . .

Fools
Off to the west in the place opposite
Damning the possibility of tides,
Screaming there are no tides in this ocean,
Pooling the past in shallow foot-prints,
Impounding the used brine. . . .

Fools
And the ship fast, the hull careened,
The planks warped by the sun, the beautiful
Carved curve of the stern in the caked

Ooze and the Minoan prow
Dribbled by roosting birds. . . .

Four thousand
Years of that sea-wandering brought to
This!
        Stalled!
                Stinking of sulphur!
Gas out of guts in the muck like voices
Blathering slanders in the house of
State, and the obscene birds, the black,
Indecent, dribbling, obscene birds,
Their mouths filled with excrement, shrieking,
Fouling the figure of the prow. . . .

The springs of the sea, O God, where are they?

Where shall the slavered eyes be washed with
Salt, the ears with salt, the tongues
Washed with the sea-salt?

                On what tide
Rising to what fresh wind, what cries
Of morning seagulls, shall the ship move;
Stir in her stench of ooze and lift
And on the cold sea, on the cleansing water,
Lean to her course?

                Where are the fountains?

Waked by the pale pink
Intimation to the eastward,
Cock, the prey of every beast,
Takes breath upon the hen-house rafter,
Leans above the fiery brink
And shrieks in brazen obscene burst
On burst of uncontrollable derisive laughter:
Cock has seen the sun! He first! He first!

REASONS FOR MUSIC

for Wallace Stevens

Why do we labor at the poem
Age after Age — even an age like
This one, when the living rock
No longer lives and the cut stone perishes? —

Hölderlin's question. Why be poet
Now when the meanings do not mean? —
When the stone shape is shaped stone? —
Dürftiger Zeit? — time without inwardness?

Why lie upon our beds at night
Holding a mouthful of words, exhausted
Most by the absence of the adversary?

Why be poet? Why be man!

Far out in the uttermost Andes
Mortised enormous stones are piled.
What is man? Who founds a poem
In the rubble of wild world — wilderness.

The acropolis of eternity that crumbles
Time and again is mine — my task.
The heart's necessity compels me:
Man I am: poet must be.

The labor of order has no rest:
To impose on the confused, fortuitous
Flowing away of the world, Form —
Still, cool, clean, obdurate,

Lasting forever, or at least
Lasting: a precarious monument
Promising immortality, for the wing
Moves and in the moving balances.

Why do we labor at the poem?
Out of the turbulence of the sea,
Flower by brittle flower, rises
The coral reef that calms the water.

Generations of the dying
Fix the sea's dissolving salts
In stone, still trees, their branches immovable,
Meaning
       the movement of the sea.